Vegan & Vegetarian Air Fryer Cookbook

Easy & Delicious Best Air Fryer Vegan & Vegetarian Recipes ideas in 2021

Beck Wall

Copyright © 2021 by Beck Wall

Table of Contents

MEDITERRANEAN VEGGIE MIX

Cook time: 20 minutes

Servings: 4

INGREDIENTS

1 large zucchini, sliced

1 green pepper, sliced

1 large parsnip, peeled and cubed

Salt and black pepper to taste

2 tablespoons honey

2 cloves garlic, crushed

1 teaspoon mixed herbs

1 teaspoon mustard

6 tablespoons olive oil, divided

4 cherry tomatoes

1 medium carrot, peeled and cubed

INSTRUCTIONS

Add the zucchini, green pepper, parsnip, cherry tomatoes, carrot to bottom of air fryer.

Cover ingredients with 3 tablespoons of oil and adjust the time to 15-minutes. Cook at 360°Fahrenheit.

Prepare your marinade by combining remaining ingredients in air fryer safe baking dish.

Combine marinade and vegetables in baking dish and stir well. Sprinkle with salt and pepper.

Cook it at 390°Fahrenheit for 5-minutes.

Breakfast Beet & Feta Salad

Cook time: 65 minutes

Servings: 4

INGREDIENTS

¾ cup of crumbled feta cheese

2 cups mixed baby spinach

½ teaspoon thyme leaves, minced

1 teaspoon marjoram, fresh, minced

1 teaspoon parsley, fresh, minced

½ tablespoon liquid Stevia

1 ½ teaspoons Dijon mustard

2 cloves of minced garlic

¼ cup red onion, minced

3 tablespoons red wine vinegar

Salt and pepper to taste

2 tablespoons olive oil

7 large beets, stems trimmed

Pistachios for garnishing

INSTRUCTIONS

Preheat your air fryer to 390°Fahrenheit. Wash the beets and dry them.

Place beets on piece of aluminum foil and add to a baking sheet.

Drizzle with oil and bake for 20-minutes in oven. Season with salt and pepper.

Transfer beets to air fryer and cook for an additional 45-minutes.

Remove them from air fryer and place in fridge. In a mixing bowl, combine onion, garlic, stevia, and mustard. Whisk these ingredients until they are well blended.

Stir in the herbs and season with salt and pepper.

When the beets are chilled, cut them into half-inch slices.

Garnish with lettuce and pistachios.

Potato Omelet

Prep time: 10 – 20 minutes

Cook time: 15 – 30 minutes

Servings: 6

INGREDIENTS

- 600 g of potatoes
- ½ onion
- 6 eggs
- Salt, pepper to taste

INSTRUCTIONS

1. Peel the potatoes and cut them into squares of approximately 1 cm; Peel the onion and cut it into slices that are not very thin.
2. Pour the onion, oil and potatoes in the basket Cook for 25 minutes at 1600C.
3. Distribute potatoes and onion well in the bottom of the basket. Then pour the previously made egg, salt, and pepper mixture. Continue cooking for another 5 minutes.

Roasted Vegetables

Cook time: 30 minutes

Servings: 4

INGREDIENTS

2 cups yellow squash, sliced

½ teaspoon salt

½ teaspoon pepper

1 tablespoon thyme leaves

1 tablespoon oregano, chopped

2 tablespoons olive oil

1 cup carrots, sliced

INSTRUCTIONS

In a bowl, add zucchini, squash, and carrots. Add oregano, oil, and thyme.
Season with pepper and salt. Toss well.
Place vegetables in air fryer basket and cook for 400°Fahrenheit for 30-minutes.

Strapatsada

Prep time: 10-20 minutes

Cook time: 15-30 minutes

Servings: 4

INGREDIENTS

- ½ onion
- 1 red pepper
- 100g mushrooms
- 300 g of tomatoes
- 6 eggs
- Fine salt to taste
- Black pepper to taste

INSTRUCTIONS

1. Cut the mushrooms (washed) and onions in julienne.
2. Distribute everything in the tank with the oil.
3. Set the temperature to 180oC and Cook for 12 minutes.
4. Add the tomatoes (skinless) cut into pieces, salt, and cook for another 8 minutes.
5. Remove the trowel (take care that it is hot!) And distribute the vegetables at the basket.
6. In a bowl, beat the eggs with salt and pepper and pour all over the vegetables. Cook another 7 to 8 minutes.

Garlic Mushrooms

Prep time: 10 minutes

Cook time: 10 minutes

Servings: 2

INGREDIENTS

- 1 slice of white bread
- 1 crushed garlic clove
- 1 tbsp chopped parsley
- Freshly ground black pepper
- 1 tbsp olive oil
- 12 mushrooms

INSTRUCTIONS

1. Preheat the air fryer to 200°C.
2. Grate the slice of bread until it is thin in the kitchen robot and mix it with the garlic, parsley, and season to taste. Finally, pour the olive oil.
3. Remove the mushroom stems and fill the caps with the breadcrumbs.
4. Place the mushrooms in the basket and place it in the air fryer. Set the timer to 10 minutes. Bake until golden brown and crispy.
5. Serve them on a tray.

Zucchini Caprese Rollups

Prep time: 5 minutes

Cook time: 8 minutes

Servings: 8

INGREDIENTS

- 1 Zucchini, sliced thinly lengthwise
- 4 oz mozzarella cheese, sliced
- 1 tomato, sliced
- 2 Tbsp chopped fresh basil
- 2 Tbsp olive oil

INSTRUCTIONS

1. Preheat your air fryer to 400 degrees F and prepare a large baking dish with foil.
2. Lay the zucchini slices out on a clean work surface.
3. Place a piece of tomato, cheese and a little basil on each zucchini slice and then roll up to enclose the filling.
4. Secure using a toothpick and then place the eggplant rolls on the prepared foil lined baking dish.
5. Drizzle with the olive oil and place in the air fryer to cook for 8 minutes. The zucchini should be lightly brown and the cheese melted. Serve warm.

ROASTED ORANGE CAULIFLOWER

Cook time: 20 minutes

Servings: 2

INGREDIENTS

- 1 head cauliflower
- ½ lemon, juiced
- ½ tablespoon olive oil
- 1 teaspoon curry powder
- Sea salt and black pepper to taste

INSTRUCTIONS

1. Prepare your cauliflower by washing and removing the leaves and core. Slice it into florets of comparable size. Grease your air fryer with oil and preheat it for 2-minutes at 390°Fahrenheit. Combine fresh lemon juice and curry powder, add the cauliflower florets and stir. Use salt and pepper as seasoning and stir again. Cook for 20-minutes and serve warm.

Mini peppers with Goat Cheese

Prep time: 10 minutes

Cook time: 8 minutes

Servings: 4

INGREDIENTS

- 8 mini peppers
- ½ tbsp olive oil
- ½ tbsp dried Italian herbs
- 1 tsp freshly ground black pepper
- 100 g soft goat cheese in eight portions

INSTRUCTIONS

1. Preheat the air fryer to 200°C.
2. Cut the top of the mini peppers and remove the seeds and the membrane.
3. Mix the olive oil in a deep dish with the Italian herbs and pepper. Pour the portions of goat cheese in the oil.
4. Press a serving of goat cheese against each mini pepper and place the mini peppers in the basket next to each other. Insert the basket in the air fryer and set the timer to 8 minutes. Bake the mini peppers until the cheese is melted.
5. Serve mini peppers in small dishes such as snacks or snacks.

SPINACH SAMOSA

Cook time: 15 minutes

Servings: 2

INGREDIENTS

1 ½ cups of almond flour

½ teaspoon baking soda

1 teaspoon garam masala

1 teaspoon coriander, chopped

¼ cup green peas

½ teaspoon sesame seeds

¼ cup potatoes, boiled, small chunks

2 tablespoons olive oil

¾ cup boiled and blended spinach puree

Salt and chili powder to taste

INSTRUCTIONS

In a bowl, mix baking soda, salt, and flour to make the dough.

Add 1-tablespoon of oil. Add the spinach puree and mix until the dough is smooth.

Place in fridge for twenty-minutes. In the pan add one tablespoon of oil, then add potatoes, peas and cook for 5-minutes.

Add the sesame seeds, garam masala, coriander, and stir.

Knead the dough and make the small ball using a rolling pin.

Form balls, make into cone shapes, which are then filled with stuffing that is not yet fully cooked.

Make sure flour sheets are well sealed.

Preheat air fryer to 390°Fahrenheit.

Place samosa in air fryer basket and cook for 10-minutes.

Sautéed Potatoes and Pumpkin

Prep time: 10 – 20 minutes

Cook time: 15 – 30 minutes

Servings: 4

INGREDIENTS

- 450 g of potatoes
- 550 g pumpkin
- 20 g of breadcrumbs
- Coarse salt

INSTRUCTIONS

1. Preheat the air fryer to 1800C for 5 minutes.
2. Thoroughly clean the pumpkin and potatoes and cut them into large pieces. Pour all ingredients into the basket.
3. Cook for 30 minutes or until you get the crispy you want.

CHIPS

Prep time: 10-20 minutes

Cook time: 30-45 minutes

Servings: 8

INGREDIENTS

- 1500g of fresh potatoes
- Fine salt to taste
- 1 tsp peanut oil

INSTRUCTIONS

1. Peel the potatoes and cut them into sticks of approximately 1 cm per side.
2. Put the cut potatoes in water for a few minutes and rinse thoroughly.
3. Drain and clean well with a paper towel.
4. Pour the potatoes and the correct amount of oil in the pan.
5. Cook for 37/40 minutes at 1800C. Salt then serve.

Eggplant Tahini Rollups

Prep time: 5 minutes

Cook time: 8 minutes

Servings: 8

INGREDIENTS

- 1 eggplant, sliced thinly lengthwise
- 4 oz mozzarella cheese, sliced
- ¼ cup tahini paste
- 2 Tbsp chopped fresh basil
- 2 Tbsp olive oil

INSTRUCTIONS

1. Preheat your air fryer to 400 degrees F and prepare a large baking dish with foil.
2. Lay the eggplant slices out on a clean work surface.
3. Spread tahini on each eggplant then top with a slice of cheese and a little basil on each eggplant slice and then roll up to enclose the filling.
4. Secure using a toothpick and then place the eggplant rolls on the prepared foil lined baking dish.
5. Drizzle with the olive oil and place in the air fryer to cook for 8 minutes. The eggplant should be lightly brown and the cheese melted. Serve warm.

Roasted Broccoli Salad

Prep time: 7 minutes

Cook time: 15 minutes

Servings: 4

INGREDIENTS

- 1 pound chopped broccoli florets
- 1 tsp minced, fresh rosemary
- ¼ cup olive oil
- 2 Tbsp balsamic vinegar
- ½ tsp Dijon mustard
- ½ tsp kosher salt

INSTRUCTIONS

1. Preheat your air fryer to 450 degrees F and line the air fryer tray or baking pan with foil.
2. Toss the chopped broccoli with the rosemary and olive oil and place on the prepared tray.
3. Roast in the air fryer for 15 minutes.
4. Place the hot, roasted sprouts in a large bowl and add the remaining ingredients to make a dressing. Toss well and serve hot or cold.

EGGPLANT CAPRESE ROLLUPS

Prep time: 5 minutes

Cook time: 8 minutes

Servings: 8

INGREDIENTS

- 1 eggplant, sliced thinly lengthwise
- 4 oz mozzarella cheese, sliced
- 1 tomato, sliced
- 2 Tbsp chopped fresh basil
- 2 Tbsp olive oil

INSTRUCTIONS

1. Preheat your air fryer to 400 degrees F and prepare a large baking dish with foil.
2. Lay the eggplant slices out on a clean work surface.
3. Place a piece of tomato, cheese and a little basil on each eggplant slice and then roll up to enclose the filling.
4. Secure using a toothpick and then place the eggplant rolls on the prepared foil lined baking dish.
5. Drizzle with the olive oil and place in the air fryer to cook for 8 minutes. The eggplant should be lightly brown and the cheese melted. Serve warm.

Crispy Cheese Sticks

Cook time: 5 minutes

Servings: 4

INGREDIENTS

1 (16-ounce) package mozzarella cheese

½ teaspoon salt

1 teaspoon garlic powder

1 teaspoon onion powder

1 teaspoon cayenne pepper

1 cup breadcrumbs

1 cup almond flour

2 eggs, beaten

INSTRUCTIONS

Cut the mozzarella cheese into 3 (1/2 inch) sticks.

Add beaten eggs in small bowl. In a bowl, add flour.

In another small bowl, combine breadcrumbs, cayenne pepper, onion powder, garlic powder, and salt.

Dip cheese sticks into beaten egg, then dip into flour, then return to egg, and coat with breadcrumbs.

Place coated cheese in the fridge for 20-minutes. Preheat your air fryer to 400°Fahrenheit.

Spray air fryer basket with cooking spray.

Place the coated cheese sticks into air fryer and cook for 5-minutes.

Serve hot!

TAWA VEGGIES

Cook time: 25 minutes

Servings: 4

INGREDIENTS

¼ cup okra

2 teaspoons garam masala

1 teaspoon red chili powder

1 teaspoon amchur powder

¼ cup taro root

¼ cup potato

¼ cup eggplant

Salt to taste

Olive oil for brushing

INSTRUCTIONS

Cut potato and taro root into fries and soak in salt water for 10 minutes.

Cut okra and eggplant into four pieces. Rinse potatoes and taro root and pat dry.

Add the spices to potatoes, taro roots, okra, and eggplant.

Brush pan with oil and preheat to 390°Fahrenheit and cook for 10-minutes.

Lower the heat to 355°Fahrenheit and cook for an additional 15-minutes.

Lemony Green Beans

Cook time: 12 minutes

Servings: 4

INGREDIENTS

- 1 lb. green beans washed and destemmed
- Sea salt and black pepper to taste
- 1 lemon
- ¼ teaspoon extra virgin olive oil

INSTRUCTIONS

1. Preheat your air fryer to 400°Fahrenheit. Place the green beans in the air fryer basket. Squeeze lemon over beans and season with salt and pepper. Cover ingredients with oil and toss well. Cook green beans for 12-minutes and serve!

Crispy Kale Chips

Cook time: 3 minutes

Servings: 2

INGREDIENTS

1 head of kale

1 teaspoon soy sauce

1 tablespoon olive oil

INSTRUCTIONS

Tear up kale into 1 ½-inch pieces. Wash clean and dry thoroughly.

Toss with olive oil and soy sauce. Fry in air fryer at 390°Fahrenheit for 3-minutes.

Eggplant Zucchini Rollups

Prep time: 5 minutes
Cook time: 8 minutes
Servings: 8

INGREDIENTS

- 1 eggplant, sliced thinly lengthwise
- 4 oz mozzarella cheese, sliced
- 1 zucchini, sliced lengthwise
- 2 Tbsp chopped fresh basil
- 2 Tbsp olive oil

INSTRUCTIONS

1. Preheat your air fryer to 400 degrees F and prepare a large baking dish with foil.
2. Lay the eggplant slices out on a clean work surface.
3. Place a piece of zucchini, cheese and a little basil on each eggplant slice and then roll up to enclose the filling.
4. Secure using a toothpick and then place the eggplant rolls on the prepared foil lined baking dish.
5. Drizzle with the olive oil and place in the air fryer to cook for 8 minutes. The eggplant should be lightly brown and the cheese melted. Serve warm.

Spicy Eggplant Rollups

Prep time: 5 minutes

Cook time: 8 minutes

Servings: 8

INGREDIENTS

- 1 eggplant, sliced thinly lengthwise
- 4 oz parmesan cheese, sliced
- 1 tomato, sliced
- 2 Tbsp chopped fresh basil
- 2 Tbsp olive oil
- 1 tsp cayenne pepper

INSTRUCTIONS

1. Preheat your air fryer to 400 degrees F and prepare a large baking dish with foil.
2. Lay the eggplant slices out on a clean work surface.
3. Place a piece of tomato, cheese and a little basil on each eggplant slice and then roll up to enclose the filling.
4. Secure using a toothpick and then place the eggplant rolls on the prepared foil lined baking dish.
5. Drizzle with the olive oil, sprinkle with the cayenne and place in the air fryer to cook for 8 minutes. The eggplant should be lightly brown and the cheese melted. Serve warm.

TASTY TOFU

Cook time: 12 minutes

Servings: 4

INGREDIENTS

¼ cup cornmeal

15-ounces extra firm tofu, drained, cubed

Salt and pepper to taste

1 teaspoon chili flakes

¾ cup cornstarch

INSTRUCTIONS

Line the air fryer basket with aluminum foil and brush with oil.

Preheat your air fryer to 370°Fahrenheit.

Mix all ingredients in a bowl. Place in air fryer and cook for 12-minutes.

Keto Pizza

Prep time: 20 minutes

Cook time: 20 minutes

Servings: 3

INGREDIENTS

- 1 cup almond flour
- 1 egg
- 3 Tbsp water
- 1 tsp minced garlic
- 1 Tbsp fresh chopped basil
- 4 Tbsp fresh grated parmesan
- ¼ cup keto tomato sauce
- ½ cup fresh diced mozzarella

INSTRUCTIONS

1. Preheat your air fryer to 375 degrees F and line the air fryer tray or baking pan with foil.
2. In a medium sized bowl, mix together the almond flour and water.
3. Add the egg and parmesan to the bowl and knead into a soft dough.
4. Place the dough on the prepared tray and press into a flat circle, about ¼ inch thick. Wet your hands if needed in order to make it easier to push the dough down.
5. Spread the tomato sauce over the dough and then top with the minced garlic, fresh basil and mozzarella.
6. Place in the preheated air fryer and bake for 18 minutes or until the cheese is melted and bubbling.
7. Slice and serve

Honey Roasted Carrots

Cook time: 12 minutes

Servings: 2

INGREDIENTS

1 tablespoon honey

Salt and pepper to taste

3 cups of baby carrots

1 tablespoon olive oil

INSTRUCTIONS

In a mixing bowl, combine carrots, honey, and olive oil.

Season with salt and pepper.

Cook in air fryer at 390°Fahrenheit for 12-minutes.

Avocado Fries

Cook time: 10 minutes

Servings: 4

INGREDIENTS

1-ounce Aquafina

1 avocado, sliced

½ teaspoon salt

½ cup panko breadcrumbs

INSTRUCTIONS

Toss the panko breadcrumbs and salt together in a bowl.

Pour Aquafina into another bowl. Dredge the avocado slices in Aquafina and then panko breadcrumbs.

Arrange the slices in single layer in air fryer basket.

Air fry at 390°Fahrenheit for 10-minutes.

Citrus Yellow Beans

Cook time: 10 minutes

Servings: 2

INGREDIENTS

1 lb. yellow beans washed, and ends trimmed

1 lime, juiced

¼ teaspoon olive oil

Salt and pepper to taste

INSTRUCTIONS

Place the yellow beans in air fryer basket and pour the lime juice over beans.

Season beans with salt and pepper. Drizzle the beans with olive oil. Cook beans at 400°Fahrenheit for 10-minutes.

Eggplant Parmesan Panini

Cook time: 25 minutes

Servings: 2

INGREDIENTS

- 1 medium eggplant, cut into ½ inch slices
- ½ cup mayonnaise
- 2 tablespoons milk
- Black pepper to taste
- ½ teaspoon garlic powder
- ½ teaspoon onion powder
- 1 tablespoon dried parsley
- ½ teaspoon Italian seasoning
- ½ cup breadcrumbs
- Sea salt to taste
- Fresh basil, chopped for garnishing
- ¾ cup tomato sauce
- 2 tablespoons parmesan, grated cheese
- 2 cups grated mozzarella cheese
- 2 tablespoons olive oil
- 4 slices artisan Italian bread
- Cooking spray

INSTRUCTIONS

1. Cover both sides of eggplant with salt. Place them between sheets of paper towels. Set aside for 30-minutes to get rid of excess moisture. In a mixing bowl, combine Italian seasoning, breadcrumbs, parsley, onion powder, garlic powder and season with salt and pepper. In another small bowl, whisk mayonnaise and milk until smooth.

2. Preheat your air fryer to 400°Fahrenheit. Remove the excess salt from eggplant slices. Cover both sides of eggplant with mayonnaise mixture. Press the eggplant slices into the breadcrumb mixture. Use cooking spray on both sides of eggplant slices. Air fry slices in batches for 15-minutes, turning over when halfway done. Each bread slice must be greased with olive oil. On a cutting board, place two slices of bread with oiled sides down. Layer mozzarella cheese and grated parmesan cheese. Place eggplant on cheese. Cover with tomato sauce and add remaining mozzarella and parmesan cheeses. Garnish with chopped fresh basil. Put the second slice of bread oiled side up on top. Take preheated Panini press and place sandwiches on it. Close the lid and cook for 10-minutes. Slice panini into halves and serve.

CHEESEY STROMBOLI

Prep time: 5 minutes

Cook time: 15 minutes

Servings: 4

INGREDIENTS

- 1 ¼ cups grated mozzarella cheese
- 4 Tbsp almond flour
- 3 Tbsp coconut flour
- 1 egg
- 1 tsp dried basil
- ¼ cup sliced mozzarella cheese
- ½ cup grated cheddar cheese

INSTRUCTIONS

1. Preheat your air fryer to 400 degrees F.
2. Melt the grated mozzarella in a large bowl using the microwave, stirring occasionally.
3. Add the flours and dried basil to the bowl with the mozzarella and mix together for one minute.
4. Add the egg and continue to mix until a nice dough forms.
5. Place the dough on a piece of parchment and then roll into a rectangle about 4 inches wide.
6. Place the sliced mozzarella and cheese slices on top of the dough, in the center.
7. Cover the sliced mozzarella and cheese with the dough, enclosing the filling in the center.
8. Place the Stromboli on a sheet tray and in the preheated air fryer and bake for 20 minutes. Slice and serve!

SPICY SWEET POTATO WEDGES

Cook time: 20 minutes

Servings: 2

INGREDIENTS

2 large sweet potatoes, cut into wedges

Salt and pepper to taste

1 tablespoon red pepper flakes

1 teaspoon cumin

1 teaspoon mustard powder

1 teaspoon chili powder

1 tablespoon olive oil

INSTRUCTIONS

Preheat air fryer to 350°Fahrenheit. Place your ingredients in a mixing bowl and stir well.

Add sweet potato wedges into air fryer basket and cook for 20-minutes.

Make sure to shake the basket every 5-minutes.

Air-Fried Sweet Potato Bites

Cook time: 15 minutes

Servings: 2

INGREDIENTS

2 sweet potatoes, diced

½ cup parsley, chopped

2 tablespoons honey

2 tablespoons olive oil

2 teaspoons cinnamon

1 teaspoon red chili flakes

INSTRUCTIONS

Preheat your air fryer to 350°Fahrenheit.

Add all the ingredients in a large mixing bowl and toss well.

Place the sweet potato mixture into air fryer basket.

Cook in preheated air fryer for 15-minutes.

BAKED GARLIC PARSLEY POTATOES

Cook time: 40 minutes

Servings: 3

INGREDIENTS

3 baking potatoes, washed

Parsley for garnishing

1 tablespoon olive oil

Sea salt to taste

2 garlic cloves, crushed

INSTRUCTIONS

Prepare the potatoes: make holes using a fork in them.

Season potatoes with salt and cover with garlic puree and olive oil. Layer the potatoes in the air fryer basket and cook at 390°Fahrenheit and cook for 40-minutes.

Roasted Corn

Cook time: 10 minutes

Servings: 8

INGREDIENTS

4 ears of corn

Salt and pepper to taste

3 teaspoons vegetable oil

INSTRUCTIONS

Remove the husks from corn, wash and pat them dry. Cut if needed to fit into air fryer basket.

Drizzle with vegetable oil and season with salt and pepper.

Cook at 400°Fahrenheit for 10-minutes.

Extra Cheese Pizza

Prep time: 20 minutes

Cook time: 20 minutes

Servings: 3

INGREDIENTS

- 1 cup almond flour
- 1 egg
- 3 Tbsp water
- 1 tsp minced garlic
- 1 Tbsp fresh chopped basil
- 4 Tbsp fresh grated parmesan
- ¼ cup keto tomato sauce
- ½ cup fresh diced mozzarella
- ½ cup shaved parmesan
- ¼ cup shredded cheddar cheese

INSTRUCTIONS

1. Preheat your air fryer to 375 degrees F and line the air fryer tray or baking pan with foil.
2. In a medium sized bowl, mix together the almond flour and water.
3. Add the egg and parmesan to the bowl and knead into a soft dough.
4. Place the dough on the prepared tray and press into a flat circle, about ¼ inch thick. Wet your hands if needed in order to make it easier to push the dough down.
5. Spread the tomato sauce over the dough and then top with the minced garlic, fresh basil, shaved parmesan, cheddar, and mozzarella.
6. Place in the preheated air fryer and bake for 18 minutes or until the cheese is melted and bubbling.
7. Slice and serve

Parmesan Potatoes

Cook time: 4 minutes

Servings: 4

INGREDIENTS

4 potatoes, diced and boiled

2 tablespoons flour

1 egg yolk

1 tablespoon olive oil

3 tablespoons breadcrumbs

Nutmeg to taste

Salt and pepper to taste

3 tablespoons parmesan cheese

INSTRUCTIONS

Mash potatoes and add all ingredients except breadcrumbs and oil to the bowl.

Mix ingredients and make into medium size balls. Mix breadcrumbs and olive oil separately.

Coat balls with breadcrumbs. Preheat air fryer to 390°Fahrenheit and cook for 4-minutes.

Eggplant Parmesan Rollups

Prep time: 5 minutes

Cook time: 8 minutes

Servings: 8

INGREDIENTS

- 1 eggplant, sliced thinly lengthwise
- 4 oz grated parmesan
- 1 tomato, sliced
- 2 Tbsp chopped fresh basil
- 2 Tbsp olive oil

INSTRUCTIONS

1. Preheat your air fryer to 400 degrees F and prepare a large baking dish with foil.
2. Lay the eggplant slices out on a clean work surface.
3. Place a piece of tomato, cheese and a little basil on each eggplant slice and then roll up to enclose the filling.
4. Secure using a toothpick and then place the eggplant rolls on the prepared foil lined baking dish.
5. Drizzle with the olive oil and place in the air fryer to cook for 8 minutes. The eggplant should be lightly brown and the cheese melted. Serve warm.

Spicy Sriracha Egg Salad

Prep time: 5 minutes

Cook time: 16 minutes

Servings: 6

INGREDIENTS

- 6 Tbsp Mayonnaise
- 8 Large Eggs
- 2 Tbsp apple cider vinegar
- 1 tsp ground black pepper
- 1 tsp salt
- 1 Tbsp sriracha sauce

INSTRUCTIONS

1. Preheat your air fryer to 250 degrees F.
2. Place a wire rack in the air fryer and place the eggs on top of the rack.
3. Cook for 16 minutes then remove the eggs and place them directly into an ice water bath to cool and stop the cooking process.
4. Peel the eggs and place in a large bowl.
5. Mash the eggs with a fork.
6. Add in the mayonnaise, cider vinegar, pepper, sriracha and salt

ONION LASAGNA

Prep time: 5 minutes

Cook time: 15 minutes

Servings: 1

INGREDIENTS

- ½ large zucchini, sliced thinly
- ¼ cup thinly sliced red onion
- 3 Tbsp keto marinara sauce
- 2 Tbsp ricotta, whole milk
- ¼ cup fresh chopped mozzarella

INSTRUCTIONS

1. Preheat your air fryer to 400 degrees F.
2. Get an oven safe large ramekin or mug.
3. Lay some of the zucchini slices and onion slices in the bottom of the cup.
4. Spread about 1 tablespoon of the ricotta on top of the zucchini then top with a tablespoon of the marinara sauce.
5. Layer more zucchini and onion on top of the marinara and repeat the layering process until you have used all the zucchini, onion ricotta and marinara.
6. Top with the mozzarella.
7. Place the lasagna in the oven and bake for 15 minutes or until the mozzarella is melted and bubbly. Enjoy hot

Couscous with Vegetables

Prep time: 10-20 minutes

Cook time: 30-45 minutes

Servings: 8

INGREDIENTS

- 50g carrot
- Eggplant 250g
- 50g cherry tomatoes
- 1 shallot
- 150g broth
- 250g zucchini
- Salt to taste
- 1 clove garlic
- Chili pepper
- 375g couscous
- 400 ml of water
- Butter taste
- 1 ml of olive oil

INSTRUCTIONS

1. Peel the garlic, cut the chili into pieces, chop the shallot and place everything on the baking sheet, distributing it well through the bottom; add the oil. Before you start cooking, wash, and cut eggplants, zucchini, carrots, and small diced tomatoes (the latter should be reserved as they will be added to couscous when they are cold).

2. Set the air fryer to 1500C and brown for 3 minutes. Add carrots, broth, and simmer for another 6 min. Finally pour the eggplant and zucchini, salt and pepper and simmer for another 25 minutes.

3. In addition to preparing the semolina by putting the water in a saucepan, boil, pour a small spoonful of salt. Add the couscous in the rain, oil, mix and stop the fire. Let swell for 3 min. Add a pinch of butter and cook again for another 3 min. mixing regularly with a fork to shell properly.

4. As soon as the vegetables have cooled, add the small tomatoes, and pour everything into a bowl with the couscous.

SPICY EGG SALAD

Prep time: 5 minutes

Cook time: 16 minutes

Servings: 6

INGREDIENTS

- 6 Tbsp Mayonnaise
- 8 Large Eggs
- 2 Tbsp apple cider vinegar
- 1 tsp ground black pepper
- 1 tsp salt
- ¼ tsp paprika
- 1 tsp cayenne pepper, ground

INSTRUCTIONS

1. Preheat your air fryer to 250 degrees F.
2. Place a wire rack in the air fryer and place the eggs on top of the rack.
3. Cook for 16 minutes then remove the eggs and place them directly into an ice water bath to cool and stop the cooking process.
4. Peel the eggs and place in a large bowl.
5. Mash the eggs with a fork.
6. Add in the mayonnaise, cider vinegar, pepper, cayenne, paprika and salt

BROCCOLI AND GRITS

Prep time: 20 minutes

Cook time: 23 minutes

Servings: 4

INGREDIENTS

- ½ pound chopped broccoli florets
- 1 Tbsp minced garlic
- 1 Tbsp fresh chopped rosemary
- ½ cup chopped pecans
- 2 Tbsp olive oil
- 2 cups chopped cauliflower florets
- 1 cup heavy cream
- ½ cup water
- 1 cup shredded cheddar cheese
- 2 Tbsp butter
- 1 tsp salt
- ¼ tsp ground black pepper

INSTRUCTIONS

1. Preheat your air fryer to 400 degrees F and line the air fryer tray or baking pan with foil.
2. Place the broccoli, garlic, rosemary, olive oil and pecans on the tray and toss to coat everything in the oil.
3. Place the tray in the air fryer and cook for 15 minutes.
4. While the broccoli is cooking, place the cauliflower in a blender or food processor and pulse until the cauliflower is like rice.
5. Place the cauliflower in a pot along with the water and cook over medium heat for 5 minutes.
6. Add the heavy cream and cook for another 3 minutes.
7. Stir in the cheese, butter, salt and pepper and mix to melt the cheese.
8. Divide between bowls and top with the roasted mushrooms. Enjoy hot!

CRISPY ONION RINGS

Cook time: 10 minutes

Servings: 2

INGREDIENTS

1 teaspoon baking powder

¾ cup breadcrumbs

1 cup milk

1 egg, beaten

1 large onion, sliced

1 teaspoon salt

1 ¼ cup almond flour

INSTRUCTIONS

Preheat the air fryer for 5-minutes. Combine the baking powder, flour, and salt in a small bowl.

Use a different bowl to whisk the egg and milk in. Place the breadcrumbs in another bowl.

Coat onion slices with flour, dip in egg mixture and coat with breadcrumbs.

Place coated onion rings into air fryer basket and cooked at 350°Fahrenheit for 10-minutes.

Serve and enjoy!

Air-Fried Crispy Zucchini

Cook time: 20 minutes

Servings: 6

INGREDIENTS

4 egg whites

6 medium zucchinis, thinly sliced

4 tablespoons parmesan cheese, grated

½ teaspoon garlic powder

1 cup breadcrumbs

Salt and pepper to taste

INSTRUCTIONS

Preheat your air fryer to 400°Fahrenheit.

Whisk salt, pepper and egg whites in small bowl. In another bowl, combine garlic powder, breadcrumbs, and parmesan cheese.

Dip zucchini slices into egg whites then coat them with breadcrumbs.

Place coated zucchini in air fryer basket and cook for 20-minutes.

CHICORY STRUDEL

Prep time: 10-20 minutes

Cook time: 30-45 minutes

Servings: 6

INGREDIENTS

- 1 puff pastry
- Red chicory
- 100 g of stravecchio cheese
- 100 g of cow mozzarella
- 3 slices of Italian stuffed piglet

INSTRUCTIONS

1. Unroll the puff pastry, cover with a layer of cheese shavings, add the pieces of raw chicory and diced mozzarella.
2. Cover the whole with slices of stuffed piglet and close the puff pastry to form a stake.
3. Place the lining on the baking paper inside the basket.
4. Set the temperature to 1600C and cook for 35 minutes.
5. Very good with cheese sauce.

Spanish Potatoes

Prep time: 10 minutes

Cook time: 57 minutes

Servings: 2

INGREDIENTS

- 400 g potato
- Water
- 1 tbsp olive oil
- Salt

INSTRUCTIONS

1. Peel and cut the potato in julienne about 0.5 CM thick.
2. Prepare a bowl with very cold water, if necessary, add ice. Place the cut potatoes for at least 30 minutes to make them starch.
3. Dry each potato with an absorbent napkin and place in another dry bowl.
4. When they are all dry, sprinkle with oil or brush with olive oil and season with salt and whatever you like (sweet paprika, oregano, etc.).
5. In this case place in a fryer without oil at temperature 1600C for 17 minutes.
6. Set the fryer at 1800C another 10 minutes and that's it.

Spicy Pepper Lasagna

Prep time: 5 minutes

Cook time: 15 minutes

Servings: 1

INGREDIENTS

- ½ large zucchini, sliced thinly
- ¼ cup chopped red bell peppers
- 3 Tbsp keto marinara sauce
- 2 Tbsp ricotta, whole milk
- ¼ cup fresh chopped mozzarella

INSTRUCTIONS

1. Preheat your air fryer to 400 degrees F.
2. Get an oven safe large ramekin or mug.
3. Lay some of the zucchini slices and chopped bell peppers in the bottom of the cup.
4. Spread about 1 tablespoon of the ricotta on top of the zucchini then top with a tablespoon of the marinara sauce.
5. Layer more zucchini and peppers on top of the marinara and repeat the layering process until you have used all the zucchini, peppers ricotta and marinara.
6. Top with the mozzarella.
7. Place the lasagna in the oven and bake for 15 minutes or until the mozzarella is melted and bubbly. Enjoy hot

Tomato Lasagna

Prep time: 5 minutes

Cook time: 15 minutes

Servings: 1

INGREDIENTS

- ½ large zucchini, sliced thinly
- ½ cup sliced cherry tomatoes
- 3 Tbsp keto marinara sauce
- 2 Tbsp ricotta, whole milk
- ¼ cup fresh chopped mozzarella

INSTRUCTIONS

1. Preheat your air fryer to 400 degrees F.
2. Get an oven safe large ramekin or mug.
3. Lay some of the zucchini slices in the bottom of the cup and top with a few tomato slices.
4. Spread about 1 tablespoon of the ricotta on top of the zucchini and tomatoes then top with a tablespoon of the marinara sauce.
5. Layer more zucchini and tomatoes on top of the marinara and repeat the layering process until you have used all the zucchini, tomatoes, ricotta and marinara.
6. Top with the mozzarella.
7. Place the lasagna in the oven and bake for 15 minutes or until the mozzarella is melted and bubbly. Enjoy hot

Crispy & Crunchy Baby Corn

Cook time: 10 minutes

Servings: 4

INGREDIENTS

1 cup almond flour

1 teaspoon garlic powder

¼ teaspoon chili powder

4 baby corns, boiled

Salt to taste

½ teaspoon carom seeds

Pinch of baking soda

INSTRUCTIONS

In a bowl, add flour, chili powder, garlic powder, baking soda, carom seed, and salt.

Mix well. Pour a little water into the batter to make a nice batter.

Dip boiled baby corn into the batter to coat.

Preheat your air fryer to 350°Fahrenheit.

Line the air fryer basket with foil and place the baby corns on foil.

Cook baby corns for 10-minutes.

Spicy Nuts

Cook time: 4 minutes

Servings: 8

INGREDIENTS

2 cups mixed nuts

1 teaspoon chipotle chili powder

1 teaspoon salt

1 teaspoon pepper

1 tablespoon butter, melted

1 teaspoon ground cumin

INSTRUCTIONS

In a bowl, add all ingredients and toss to coat.

Preheat your air fryer to 350°Fahrenheit for 5-minutes.

Add mixed nuts into air fryer basket and roast for 4-minutes.

SPICY POTATOES

Prep time: 10-20 minutes

Cook time: 30-45 minutes

Servings: 8

INGREDIENTS

- 1250g of fresh potatoes
- 10g sweet paprika
- Tomato puree
- 2 tbsp vinegar
- Salt and pepper to taste

INSTRUCTIONS

1. Peel the potatoes and cut them into 1 cm cubes on each side. Put the potatoes in the water for a few minutes and rinse them well. Drain and clean with a paper towel.
2. Pour the potatoes, rosemary, and the exact amount of oil inside the tank, salt, and pepper.
3. Set the air fryer to 1600C and cook for 25 min.
4. Add the paprika, tomato puree and vinegar, then finish cooking and simmer for another 10 minutes.
5. Prepare the "tapas" by piercing the potatoes with toothpicks.

Mediterranean Bream

Prep time: 10-20 minutes

Cook time: 15-30 minutes

Servings: 2

INGREDIENTS

- 2 gold
- 200g cherry tomatoes
- 100g of black olives
- 1 clove garlic
- Thyme to taste
- Leaves to taste
- Pepper to taste
- 1 tsp peanut oil

INSTRUCTIONS

1. First, remove the golden scales. Clean them and gut them. Salt and pepper inside the belly, add a clove of garlic and two sprigs of thyme.
2. Grease the basket with the oil.
3. Cut the tomatoes in half and add them to the basket with the black olives and capers; salt everything
4. Set the temperature to 1500C and cook for 25 minutes.

Toast with Eggplant Caviar

Prep time: 10-20 minutes

Cook time: 15-30 minutes

Servings: 8

INGREDIENTS

- Eggplants 450g
- 1 tbsp concentrated tomatoes
- 100 g almonds
- 1 shallot
- 25 g of Parmesan
- 15 basil leaves
- Bread slices

INSTRUCTIONS

1. Cut the shallot finely and pour it into the basket previously greased with the spray.
2. Brown for 2 minutes at 1600C.
3. Add chopped eggplants, tomato puree diluted in 100 ml of water, salt and cook for 23 minutes.
4. Chill the eggplants after cooking. Place the almonds in the basket and roast them for 4 to 5 minutes.
5. Mix eggplant with almonds, parmesan, and basil separately until a homogeneous compound is obtained.
6. Remove the preparation paddle from the tank (be careful, it will be hot), place the slices of bread inside and roast them for 4 to 5 minutes or until golden brown.
7. Fill each crust with the previously prepared sauce.

LEMON EGGPLANT ROLLUPS

Prep time: 5 minutes

Cook time: 8 minutes

Servings: 8

INGREDIENTS

- 1 eggplant, sliced thinly lengthwise
- 4 oz mozzarella cheese, sliced
- 2 Tbsp chopped fresh basil
- 2 Tbsp olive oil
- 1 tsp lemon zest

INSTRUCTIONS

1. Preheat your air fryer to 400 degrees F and prepare a large baking dish with foil.
2. Lay the eggplant slices out on a clean work surface.
3. Place a piece of tomato, cheese and a little basil on each eggplant slice and then roll up to enclose the filling.
4. Secure using a toothpick and then place the eggplant rolls on the prepares foil lined baking dish.
5. Drizzle with the olive oil, sprinkle with the lemon zest and place in the air fryer to cook for 8 minutes. The eggplant should be lightly brown and the cheese melted. Serve warm.

AIR FRYER ASPARAGUS

Cook time: 10 minutes

Servings: 4

INGREDIENTS

10 asparagus spears,
woody ends chopped off

Salt and pepper to taste

1 garlic clove, minced

4 tablespoons olive oil

INSTRUCTIONS

Preheat air fryer to 400°Fahrenheit for 5-minutes.

Combine the garlic and oil in a bowl.

Coat the asparagus with oil mixture and place it into air fryer basket.

Season asparagus with salt and pepper and cook for 10-minutes.

Roasted Squash Grits

Prep time: 20 minutes

Cook time: 23 minutes

Servings: 4

INGREDIENTS

- ½ pound chopped butternut squash
- 1 Tbsp minced garlic
- 1 Tbsp fresh chopped rosemary
- ½ cup chopped walnuts
- 2 Tbsp olive oil
- 2 cups chopped cauliflower florets
- 1 cup heavy cream
- ½ cup water
- 1 cup shredded cheddar cheese
- 2 Tbsp butter
- 1 tsp salt
- ¼ tsp ground black pepper

INSTRUCTIONS

1. Preheat your air fryer to 400 degrees F and line the air fryer tray or baking pan with foil.
2. Place the butternut squash, garlic, rosemary, olive oil and walnuts on the tray and toss to coat everything in the olive oil.
3. Place the tray in the air fryer and cook for 15 minutes.
4. While the squash is cooking, place the cauliflower in a blender or food processor and pulse until the cauliflower is like rice.
5. Place the cauliflower in a pot along with the water and cook over medium heat for 5 minutes.
6. Add the heavy cream and cook for another 3 minutes.
7. Stir in the cheese, butter, salt and pepper and mix to melt the cheese.
8. Divide between bowls and top with the roasted mushrooms. Enjoy hot!

Carrots with Cumin

Cook time: 12 minutes

Servings: 4

INGREDIENTS

2 cups carrots, peeled and chopped

¼ cup coriander

1 tablespoon olive oil

1 teaspoon cumin

INSTRUCTIONS

Coat the carrots with cumin and oil. Cook at 390°Fahrenheit for 12-minutes. Sprinkle with coriander over the carrots. Serve and enjoy!

Air-Grilled Tomatoes

Cook time: 20 minutes

Servings: 2

INGREDIENTS

2 tomatoes

Salt and pepper to taste

Herbs of choice

Cooking spray

INSTRUCTIONS

Cut the tomatoes in half. Spray the bottoms of them lightly with cooking spray.

Turn all halves cut side up. Spray lightly with cooking spray.

Sprinkle with ground black pepper and your choice of dried herbs, such as oregano, parsley, basil, sage, thyme, etc.

Place the tomato halves on the top tray of air fryer with cut-side up.

Turn air fryer to 320°Fahrenheit for 20 minutes.

Air-Fried Baked Potatoes

Cook time: 20 minutes

Servings: 4

INGREDIENTS

4 potatoes

Salt and pepper to taste

Olive oil as needed

INSTRUCTIONS

Peel potatoes then cut them in half. Preheat your air fryer to 355°Fahrenheit.
Brush potatoes gently with oil then cook in preheated air fryer for 10-minutes.
Brush again with oil and cook for another 10-minutes.

BEANS IN SAUCE

Prep time: 0-10 minutes

Cook time: 15-30 minutes

Servings: 8

INGREDIENTS

- 500g canned beans
- 300g of tomato puree
- ½ carrot
- 1 onion
- ½ sprig of rosemary
- Salt and pepper to taste
- 1 tsp olive oil

INSTRUCTIONS

1. Prepare a chopped carrot and onion and place it inside the cooking tray with rosemary. Grease the basket with the oil.
2. Set the air fryer to 1500C and brown for 4 min.
3. Add the drained beans from your vegetable water and rinse thoroughly, simmer for another 3 min.
4. Add the tomato, ½ glass of water, salt and pepper and continue cooking for another 13 minutes.

POTATO TOTS

Cook time: 8 minutes

Servings: 2

INGREDIENTS

1 large potato, diced

Salt and pepper to taste

1 teaspoon onion, minced

1 tablespoon olive oil

INSTRUCTIONS

Cover potatoes with water in saucepan and boil over medium-high heat.

Drain the potatoes and place in a bowl and mash potatoes.

Add olive oil, onion, pepper and salt to mashed potatoes and mix well.

Make small tots from potato mixture and place into air fryer basket.

Cook at 380°Fahrenheit for 8-minutes. Shake basket and cook for another 5-minutes.

Serve hot!

CHEESY BRUSSELS SPROUT SALAD

Prep time: 7 minutes

Cook time: 15 minutes

Servings: 4

INGREDIENTS

- 1 pound Brussel sprouts, sliced in quarters
- 1 tsp minced, fresh rosemary
- ¼ cup olive oil
- 1 Tbsp apple cider vinegar
- 2 Tbsp lemon juice
- ½ tsp Dijon mustard
- ½ tsp kosher salt
- ½ cup grated parmesan cheese

INSTRUCTIONS

1. Preheat your air fryer to 450 degrees F and line the air fryer tray or baking pan with foil.
2. Toss the Brussels sprouts with the rosemary and olive oil and place on the prepared tray.
3. Roast in the air fryer for 15 minutes.
4. Place the hot, roasted sprouts in a large bowl and add the remaining ingredients to make a dressing. Toss well and serve hot or cold.

Avocado Egg Salad

Prep time: 5 minutes

Cook time: 16 minutes

Servings: 6

INGREDIENTS

- 6 Tbsp Mayonnaise
- 8 Large Eggs
- 2 Tbsp apple cider vinegar
- 1 tsp ground black pepper
- 1 tsp salt
- 1 avocado, chopped

INSTRUCTIONS

1. Preheat your air fryer to 250 degrees F.
2. Place a wire rack in the air fryer and place the eggs on top of the rack.
3. Cook for 16 minutes then remove the eggs and place them directly into an ice water bath to cool and stop the cooking process.
4. Peel the eggs and place in a large bowl.
5. Mash the eggs with a fork.
6. Add in the mayonnaise, cider vinegar, pepper and salt.
7. Gently stir in the avocado and then serve chilled.

ZUCCHINI THINLY SLICED

Prep time: 0-10 minutes

Cook time: 15-30 minutes

Servings: 6

INGREDIENTS

- 600g zucchini
- 1 clove garlic
- 100 ml of water
- 1 tsp olive oil
- Parsley Taste
- Salt to taste
- Pepper to taste

INSTRUCTIONS

1. Wash and turn the zucchini, then dry them and cut them into rings. Add the oil and peeled garlic to the basket.
2. Set the temperature to 1500C.
3. Brown for about 2 minutes, then remove the garlic from the tank and pour the zucchini with the water, season with salt and pepper and close the lid.
4. Simmer for 23 minutes. At the end of cooking, add the chopped parsley, a drizzle of oil and serve.

DEVILED EGG SALAD

Prep time: 5 minutes

Cook time: 16 minutes

Servings: 6

INGREDIENTS

- 6 Tbsp Mayonnaise
- 8 Large Eggs
- 2 Tbsp apple cider vinegar
- 1 tsp ground black pepper
- 1 tsp salt
- 1 tsp smoked paprika, ground

INSTRUCTIONS

1. Preheat your air fryer to 250 degrees F.
2. Place a wire rack in the air fryer and place the eggs on top of the rack.
3. Cook for 16 minutes then remove the eggs and place them directly into an ice water bath to cool and stop the cooking process.
4. Peel the eggs and place in a large bowl.
5. Mash the eggs with a fork.
6. Add in the mayonnaise, cider vinegar, pepper, smoked paprika and salt

Mug Lasagna

Prep time: 5 minutes

Cook time: 15 minutes

Servings: 1

INGREDIENTS

- ½ large zucchini, sliced thinly
- 3 Tbsp keto marinara sauce
- 2 Tbsp ricotta, whole milk
- ¼ cup fresh chopped mozzarella

INSTRUCTIONS

1. Preheat your air fryer to 400 degrees F.
2. Get an oven safe large ramekin or mug.
3. Lay some of the zucchini slices in the bottom of the cup.
4. Spread about 1 tablespoon of the ricotta on top of the zucchini then top with a tablespoon of the marinara sauce.
5. Layer more zucchini on top of the marinara and repeat the layering process until you have used all the zucchini, ricotta and marinara.
6. Top with the mozzarella.
7. Place the lasagna in the oven and bake for 15 minutes or until the mozzarella is melted and bubbly. Enjoy hot

RICE SPAGHETTI WITH VEGETABLES

Prep time: 10 – 20 minutes

Cook time: 15 – 30 minutes

Servings: 4

INGREDIENTS

- 100 g of celery
- 150 g of carrots
- 150g kale
- 2 scallions
- 2 tbsp soy sauce
- 100 g of bean sprouts
- 200 g of rice spaghetti

INSTRUCTIONS

1. Spray the basket of the air fryer. Cut all the vegetables in julienne and put the celery, chives, and carrots in the basket.
2. Set the air fryer to 1500C. Cook for 10 minutes.
3. Add the sprouts and soy sauce and cook for another 10 minutes.
4. Meanwhile, cook the rice spaghetti in salted water and boil and serve with the previously prepared sauce.

Draniki

Prep time: 10-20 minutes

Cook time: 15-30 minutes

Servings: 2

INGREDIENTS

- 4 medium potatoes
- ½ onion
- 1 carrot
- 1 egg
- 100g flour
- Leaves to taste
- 1 tsp oil

INSTRUCTIONS

1. Peel the potatoes, the onion and the carrot and wash them well.
2. Using a food processor cut all vegetables in julienne and place them in a large bowl.
3. Add the egg, salt, and flour (the doses of the latter may vary depending on the degree of moisture present in the vegetables) and mix well.
4. Cover the bottom of the basket with baking paper and pour a little of the mixture with a tablespoon and spread well.
5. Fill the useful space inside the tank (about 5 to 6 empanadas at a time).
6. Set the air fryer to 180oC.
7. Cook for 10 to 12 minutes depending on the degree of browning desired.
8. After finishing the mixture, remove the baking paper, grease the bottom of the tank, and brown the previously cooked empanadas for another 2 minutes on each side.

Green Salad with Roasted Pepper

Prep time: 15 minutes

Cook time: 10 minutes

Servings: 4

INGREDIENTS

- 1 red pepper
- 1 tbsp lemon juice
- 3 tbsp yogurt
- 2 tbsp olive oil
- Freshly ground black pepper
- 1 romaine lettuce in wide strips
- 50 g arugula leaves

INSTRUCTIONS

1. Preheat the air fryer to 200°C.
2. Place the pepper in the basket and place it in the air fryer. Set the timer to 10 minutes and roast the pepper until the skin is slightly burned.
3. Place the pepper in a bowl and cover it with a lid or with transparent film. Let stand 10 to 15 minutes.
4. Next, cut the pepper into four parts and remove the seeds and skin. Cut the pepper into strips.
5. Mix a dressing in a bowl with 2 tablespoons of the pepper juice, lemon juice, yogurt, and olive oil. Add pepper and salt to taste.
6. Pour the lettuce and arugula leaves into the dressing and garnish the salad with the pepper strips.

Crispy Herb Cauliflower Florets

Cook time: 20 minutes

Servings: 2

INGREDIENTS

1 egg, beaten

2 tablespoons parmesan cheese, grated

2 cups cauliflower florets, boiled

¼ cup almond flour

1 tablespoon olive oil

Salt to taste

½ tablespoon mixed herbs

½ teaspoon chili powder

½ teaspoon garlic powder

½ cup breadcrumbs

INSTRUCTIONS

In a bowl, combine garlic powder, breadcrumbs, chili powder, mixed herbs, salt, and cheese.

Add olive oil to the breadcrumb mixture and mix well.

Place flour in a bowl and place the egg in another bowl.

Dip the cauliflower florets into the beaten egg, then in flour, and coat with breadcrumbs.

Preheat your air fryer to 350°Fahrenheit.

Place the coated cauliflower florets inside air fryer basket and cook for 20-minutes.

ROASTED POTATOES WITH PAPRIKA AND GREEK YOGURT

Prep time: 10 minutes

Cook time: 20 minutes

Servings: 4

INGREDIENTS

- 800 g of white potatoes
- 2 tbsp olive oil
- 1 tbsp spicy paprika
- Freshly ground black pepper
- 150 ml Greek yogurt

INSTRUCTIONS

1. Preheat the air fryer to 180oC. Peel the potatoes and cut them into cubes of 3 cm. Dip the cubes in water for at least 30 minutes. Dry them well with paper towels.

2. In a medium-sized bowl, mix 1 tablespoon of olive oil with the paprika and add pepper to taste. Coat the potato dice with the spiced oil.

3. Place the potato dice in the fryer basket and place it in the air fryer. Set the timer to 20 minutes and fry the dice until golden brown and ready to take. Spin them occasionally.

4. In a small bowl, mix the Greek yogurt with the remaining tablespoon of olive oil and add salt and pepper to taste. Spread the paprika over the mixture. Serve the yogurt as a sauce with the potatoes.

5. Serve the potato dice on a tray and salt them. They will be delicious with ribs or kebabs.

Air-Fried Potato Au Gratin

Cook time: 15 minutes

Servings: 4

INGREDIENTS

¼ cup milk

3 tablespoons cheddar cheese, grated

3 potatoes, peeled and sliced

¼ teaspoon nutmeg

¼ teaspoon pepper

¼ teaspoon salt

¼ cup coconut cream

INSTRUCTIONS

Preheat air fryer to 400°Fahrenheit.

Add the cream and milk into a bowl and season with salt, pepper, and nutmeg. Coat potato slices in milk and cream mixture.

Arrange the potato slices in an oven-safe dish and pour remaining cream on top of potato slices.

Sprinkle the top with grated cheese.

Place into air fryer basket and cook for 15-minutes.

Vol Au Vent with Mushrooms

Prep time: 10 - 20 minutes

Cook time: 15 – 30 minutes

Servings: 6

INGREDIENTS

- 1 roll of puff pastry
- Whole milk to taste
- 100 g of air sautéed mushrooms and parsley
- Brie to taste

INSTRUCTIONS

1. Unroll the puff pastry, prick the bottom with a fork and cut 18 discs about 7 cm in diameter. Place 6 discs in the bowl covered with baking paper.

2. Make a hole of approximately 3 cm in the other 12 discs and place them two at a time in the large discs. Brush with milk so that they adhere well to each other.

3. Set the temperature to 160OC

4. Cook for 15 to 17 minutes. Rotate the baking paper after 10 minutes for best results.

5. Fill the vol au vent with a preparation of mushrooms sautéed in air and parsley and cover with a piece of cheese.

6. Serve still hot

Pumpkin Seed Brown Bread

Cook time: 28 minutes

Servings: 4

INGREDIENTS

8 ounces of almond flour

1 ounce of liquid Stevia

1 egg

2 tablespoons butter

½ cup pumpkin seeds

INSTRUCTIONS

Mix all the ingredients in a bowl, except the butter and egg.

Keep mixing with hands. Add the butter and knead mixture.

Let the bread dough rest, keep it covered and warm for about 2-hours or until it doubles in size.

Once this happens, divide the dough into small balls of about 1-ounce each and place in a baking paper.

Top with pumpkin seeds. Brush the balls with the egg and allow dough to rest for 40-minutes.

Place the dough balls in a baking tray and place in air fryer at 330°Fahrenheit for 20 minutes or until brown and cooked.

Asian Broccoli Salad

Prep time: 7 minutes

Cook time: 15 minutes

Servings: 4

INGREDIENTS

- 1 pound chopped broccoli florets
- ¼ cup olive oil
- 2 Tbsp rice wine vinegar
- 2 Tbsp soy sauce
- ½ tsp red chili pepper flakes
- ½ tsp kosher salt

INSTRUCTIONS

1. Preheat your air fryer to 450 degrees F and line the air fryer tray or baking pan with foil.
2. Toss the chopped broccoli with the olive oil and place on the prepared tray.
3. Roast in the air fryer for 15 minutes.
4. Place the hot, roasted sprouts in a large bowl and add the remaining ingredients to make a dressing. Toss well and serve hot or cold.

Maple Brussels Sprout Salad

Prep time: 7 minutes

Cook time: 15 minutes

Servings: 4

INGREDIENTS

- 1 pound Brussel sprouts, sliced in quarters
- 1 tsp minced, fresh rosemary
- ¼ cup olive oil
- 1 Tbsp apple cider vinegar
- 1 tsp maple extract
- 2 Tbsp lemon juice
- ½ tsp Dijon mustard
- ½ tsp kosher salt

INSTRUCTIONS

1. Preheat your air fryer to 450 degrees F and line the air fryer tray or baking pan with foil.
2. Toss the Brussels sprouts with the rosemary and olive oil and place on the prepared tray.
3. Roast in the air fryer for 15 minutes.
4. Place the hot, roasted sprouts in a large bowl and add the remaining ingredients to make a dressing. Toss well and serve hot or cold.

Potatoes, Beets and Carrots

Prep time: 10-20 minutes

Cook time: 30-45 minutes

Servings: 6

INGREDIENTS

- 300g beet
- 300 g of carrots
- 300 g of potatoes
- 2 cloves of garlic
- Rosemary to taste
- Salt to taste
- Pepper to taste

INSTRUCTIONS

1. Clean, wash all vegetables (beets, carrots, and potatoes) and cut them into pieces of 2 to 3 cm.
2. Put the garlic clove, chopped vegetables, rosemary and spray the basket; Season with salt and pepper.
3. Cook for about 35 minutes at 1500C.

ROASTED BRUSSELS SPROUT SALAD

Prep time: 7 minutes

Cook time: 15 minutes

Servings: 4

INGREDIENTS

- 1 pound Brussel sprouts, sliced in quarters
- 1 tsp minced, fresh rosemary
- ¼ cup olive oil
- 1 Tbsp apple cider vinegar
- 2 Tbsp lemon juice
- ½ tsp Dijon mustard
- ½ tsp kosher salt

INSTRUCTIONS

1. Preheat your air fryer to 450 degrees F and line the air fryer tray or baking pan with foil.
2. Toss the Brussels sprouts with the rosemary and olive oil and place on the prepared tray.
3. Roast in the air fryer for 15 minutes.
4. Place the hot, roasted sprouts in a large bowl and add the remaining ingredients to make a dressing. Toss well and serve hot or cold.

PROVENCAL TOMATOES

Prep time: 10 – 20 minutes

Cook time: 15 – 30 minutes

Servings: 4

INGREDIENTS

- 4 tomatoes
- 80 g of breadcrumbs
- 1 clove garlic
- 2 marjoram branches
- 1 rosemary branch
- Parsley chopped to taste
- Salt to taste
- Butter to taste

INSTRUCTIONS

1. Remove the top of the tomatoes and drain them. Separately, place all other ingredients (except butter) in a bowl and mix them; The mixture must be quite sandy.
2. Fill the tomatoes and then place them in the basket by adding the butter.
3. Set the temperature to 1600C and cook for 20 minutes depending on the size of the tomatoes.
4. It can be served both cold and hot.

Rillette mushroom crusts

Prep time: more than 30,

Cook time: 15 - 30,

Calories: 273

INGREDIENTS

- 400g mushrooms
- 1 shallot
- 40g nuts without shell
- 150g of butter
- Parsley at discretion
- 1 tsp olive oil
- Bread slices

INSTRUCTIONS

1. Cut the shallot finely and pour it into the greased basket previously preheat at 1500C for 5 minutes.
2. Let brown for 2 minutes.
3. Add sliced mushrooms, salt, and cook for 20 minutes.
4. At the end of cooking, mix the mushrooms, soft butter and nuts until a homogeneous mixture is obtained.
5. Put everything in the fridge for 1 hour.
6. Remove the preparation paddle from the basket (be careful, it will be hot), place the slices of bread inside and toast them for 4 to 5 minutes or until golden brown.
7. Fill each crouton with the rillette.

Mushroom Lunch Lasagna

Prep time: 5 minutes

Cook time: 15 minutes

Servings: 1

INGREDIENTS

- ½ large zucchini, sliced thinly
- ½ cup thinly sliced mushrooms
- 3 Tbsp keto marinara sauce
- 2 Tbsp ricotta, whole milk
- ¼ cup fresh chopped mozzarella

INSTRUCTIONS

1. Preheat your air fryer to 400 degrees F.
2. Get an oven safe large ramekin or mug.
3. Lay some of the zucchini and mushroom slices in the bottom of the cup.
4. Spread about 1 tablespoon of the ricotta on top of the zucchini then top with a tablespoon of the marinara sauce.
5. Layer more zucchini and mushrooms on top of the marinara and repeat the layering process until you have used all the zucchini, mushrooms, ricotta and marinara.
6. Top with the mozzarella.
7. Place the lasagna in the oven and bake for 15 minutes or until the mozzarella is melted and bubbly. Enjoy hot

Fall Broccoli Salad

Prep time: 7 minutes

Cook time: 15 minutes

Servings: 4

INGREDIENTS

- 1 pound chopped broccoli florets
- 1 tsp minced, fresh rosemary
- ¼ tsp dried sage
- ¼ cup olive oil
- 1 tsp maple extract
- ½ tsp Dijon mustard
- ½ tsp kosher salt

INSTRUCTIONS

1. Preheat your air fryer to 450 degrees F and line the air fryer tray or baking pan with foil.
2. Toss the chopped broccoli with the rosemary, sage and olive oil and place on the prepared tray.
3. Roast in the air fryer for 15 minutes.
4. Place the hot, roasted sprouts in a large bowl and add the remaining ingredients to make a dressing. Toss well and serve hot or cold.

POTATOES AND YOGURT SAUCE

Prep time: 10 – 20 minutes

Cook time: 30 – 45 minutes

Servings: 4

INGREDIENTS

- 750 g of fresh potatoes
- 1 pepper
- 1 onion
- Salt taste
- Basil at ease
- 50 g lean yogurt
- 50 g of mayonnaise
- 20 g tomato sauce
- 1 pinch sweet paprika

INSTRUCTIONS

1. Wash the potatoes and let them soak in cold water and baking soda for 15 minutes and then brush them well with water.
2. Cut them in quarters and put them in the basket previously greased.
3. Set the air fryer to 1500C.
4. Cook the potatoes for 15 minutes and then add the chopped pepper and sliced onion; Salt.
5. Cook for another 15 minutes and then add the fresh basil cut from the menu.
6. Cook for another 15 minutes.
7. If you want to accompany the potatoes with the yogurt sauce, simply mix all the ingredients until you get a creamy sauce.

www.ingramcontent.com/pod-product-compliance
Lightning Source LLC
Chambersburg PA
CBHW081355160726
48000CB00010B/3357